WASHI

XENOGRAF

N G T O N

A Gallery of the Seasons

Photography and Essays

BRUCE HEINEMANN

Foreword

DAVID SKINNER

ISBN 0-930861-24-8

Washington: A Gallery of The Seasons.
Copyright 1995 Bruce W. Heinemann
Published by Gifts by Design
Post Office Box 99587
Seattle, Washington 98199
For information: (206) 286-6688
Fax: (206) 287-1865

Printed in Hong Kong Through Palace Press International, San Francisco, California
Thanks to Barbara Visser for fine editorial work.
Design by: TMA Ted Mader Associates, Seattle, Washington

This book is dedicated to my mother, Ruth, and the memory of my father, Harold,

for they taught us to appreciate and respect the land,

and to my son, Chase, and daugther, Jackie, to whom it will pass.

CONTENTS

FOREWORD

Through the great tradition of American photography we have a rich legacy of mirror images which enable us, as viewers, to reflect upon our culture in a profound and personal way. As we consider, for example, the development of the American West, we can vividly recall the photographs which have documented the regrettable consequences of a blind pursuit of manifest destiny. On the other hand we find inspiration in the magnificent nineteenth century stills of J.K. Hillers, Carlton Wilkins and F.J. Haynes, who have captured the grand vistas of Yosemite, Yellowstone, and the Colorado River, respectively. Equally inspiring are the collected works of Edward S. Curtis and Edward H. Latham, who recorded the vanishing vestiges of North America's indigenous peoples. F.M. Steele did his part by photographing another disappearing breed on the American landscape—the American cowboy.

Bruce Heinemann follows more in the tradition of the modern classicists: Ansel Adams, Eliot Porter, and Edward Weston. It is through the work of artists such as these that we have an opportunity to remind ourselves of the vistas, as well as the values, that brought our families to this part of the world. But with this abundance of riches, it is also important to remember the responsibility each of us shares in sustaining this natural heritage which we have collectively assumed.

In creating *Washington: A Gallery of the Seasons* Bruce has captured images from both sides of the Cascades which involve all of our senses. As we witness the four elements in their most natural condition throughout the four seasons, the photographs take us to the very soul of our American roots, as seen in the writings of Thoreau, Whitman and Frost. We can feel the subtle, seasonal shifts in much the same way that Vivaldi must have, as he composed. We see in this photographic showcase many of the same images that we relate to the canvasses of renowned Northwest painters such as Morris Graves, Mark Tobey and Richard Gilkey or even beyond to the works of Rothko, Monet or the Sumi brush painters. In an age of information highways, byways and specialization, it is refreshing to appreciate the work of someone who is an artist for all seasons. Bruce demonstrates an extraordinary ability to draw from a rich background of music, art and the printed word. The result is a body of work that speaks to both our hearts and minds.

In considering all of this I have often thought of my great grandfather, who came to this part of the world at the turn of the century in order to operate the Port Blakely sawmill, which was at the time the largest in the world. By today's standards the mill could hardly be considered a "politically correct" operation, but these are the 1990's—not the 1890's! Later, he sold the mill in order to move into the shipbuilding and salmon packing business. He clearly understood that each of these enterprises required a fundamental understanding of natural resources and to that extent he too was a modern classicist.

I cannot help but wonder what my great grandfather saw the first time he stood on the deck of the San Francisco steamer as it moved into Puget Sound or walked into the woods for the first time on the Olympic Peninsula. Fortunately, I need look no further than the images of Ashel Curtis (brother of Edward) to gain an understanding of those places in those times. Like Bruce's images, these photographs stand as a wordless and timeless record of life as it was at that time.

As I gaze out my office window across Elliott Bay to the Olympics beyond, I wonder what our forebears would think of this state today. While much of the beauty remains, it is quite clear that the economic opportunities that awaited those in the late 1800's have changed dramatically. I think that the images found in *A Gallery of the Seasons* would remind my great grandfather that there are those here today who share many of the same values that brought him to these shores as a young man. The opportunities afford a different set of challenges that asks us to sustain an environment that will provide for generations to come. It is through such stewardship that we find our true humanity. That is our vision and ultimate mission, made all the more clear when we enter the world of Bruce Heinemann in *Washington: A Gallery of the Seasons*.

DAVID SKINNER

INTRODUCTION

It had been over six hours since we had left New York on this red-eye flight to Seattle. Drifting off for only brief periods, my mind was far too engaged in planning my next photo shoot to settle down for serious sleep. I turned once more, trying to get comfortable, and pulled up the window shade in time to catch the sun, rising behind us, splash its first rays of warm light across the wing. Far below, the dark, curved outlines of rolling wheat fields undulated gently south toward the Snake River. One by one, the highest points of terrain became elliptical swatches of magenta. Thirty years earlier, and twenty-three thousand feet below, I sat atop Cougar Hill which rose behind my uncle's wheat farm in the heart of this Palouse country. My cousin and I straddled our motorcycles and basked in the fragrant, dusty warmth of the evening harvest sun. Speaking of girls and football, we gazed across the golden quilt of wheat fields which spread to Spokane in the distance; columns of dust and grain chaff rose skyward from the monstrous combines creeping along the hillsides. I remember how beautifully unreal the landscape seemed: earthly form, sunlight, and human activity became one in this visual masterpiece, this living painting.

As the plane continued its descent over the Columbia Basin, the rich and fertile mosaic of the Palouse gracefully gave way to the abstract composition of sagebrush, basalt rock outcroppings, green wetland marshes, and fields of irrigated agriculture now illuminated by the soft, early morning sunlight. The Columbia River came into view and alternately reflected colors of the sun-washed basalt cliffs and the clear sky, a luminous gold and teal skinned serpent winding its way across the vast inland plateau. I inhaled the aroma of hot coffee handed to me by the flight attendant; in my mind, I inhaled the sweet, earthy fragrance of mint, timothy alfalfa, and wheat stubble coming in the open car window as my father and I drove through the Columbia Basin on the way to my uncle's farm.

The sun continued to rise in the sky on this morning flight; its warm hues on the craggy eastern slopes of Mt. Rainier slowly transformed into the silvery blue luster of brilliant white snow. Perched on the Cascade Crest, Mt. Rainier, the majestic emperor, and his court of St. Helens, Adams, Glacier Peak, and Baker, loomed as volcanic sentinels of solitude, guardians of the alpine landscape. We flew close to the mountain and I examined the terrain against the glare, hoping that I might discern the minute forms of a climbing party making its way across the glacier to the summit.

The plane banked gently to the north, and my window became the lens of a camera, panning the distant landscapes of Southwest Washington. The open prairies and gently rolling farmlands merged almost imperceptibly with the foothills of the southern Olympic Mountains which, except for a few scattered patches of northerly exposed snow fields, revealed their jagged faces. With emerald islands laid at their feet, the Olympics towered above Hood Canal and the southern reaches of Puget Sound. Directly below me, whitecaps and rainbow sails danced on the cobalt waves. Just beyond the mountains' crest, a thick blanket of fog, brewed from moist ocean air, snuggled up against the windward slopes. Though I couldn't see them, hidden in the misty shroud, I know well the details of this rugged North Washington coast: the lush Hoh Rainforest, the glacier-scoured lakes, the pristine coastline.

As the plane leveled off for final approach, I caught a fleeting view north across Puget Sound and toward Canada, the San Juan archipelago, and the Gulf Islands. With giant-sized steps, one could hop from island to island all the way to Alaska. After the flight ended, I scrambled onto the escalator with my bags, tired but somehow renewed. No wonder, I thought, how to an uninitiated visitor, the descent into our state might seem a fantasy.

An immigrant from Russia, my great grandfather William Heinemann settled his family in Ritzville in the year 1888. Homesteading on 160 acres, the William Heinemann family began a legacy of wheat farming in Eastern Washington, carried on by their descendants today more than a century later. Although I was born and raised in Seattle, my family heritage in Ritzville brought me east of the Cascades many times every year. Some of my most pleasant childhood memories are riding motorcycles and tossing hay bales at my uncle's farm in the Palouse, following a rattlesnake's trail in the sand below Steamboat Rock, or finally getting up on one water-ski at Williams Lake. And although I didn't realize it until many years later when I picked up my first camera, those early experiences and the long hours I spent traveling across the state blessed me with a deep love and appreciation of the magnificence and unrivaled diversity of the Washington landscape. In fact, the longer I photograph here, and as I travel more often to other states and distant locations, the more I see the remarkable nature of Washington.

Our state is a landscape of dynamic contrasts. This diverse nature most clearly manifests in the two distinct climates and landscapes that exist on the leeward and windward sides of the Cascade Mountains. Much of the unique visual character of Washington derives from the powerful and ancient geologic forces that shaped the face of this land. The volcanic force of the Cascades combined with the power of glaciers from the last ice-age to sculpt a masterpiece of coulees, basalt cliffs, and desert plateaus in the eastern region. West of the Cascades, glaciers also carved the physical features of the inland landscape. Advancing south, the vast sheets of rock and ice scoured the terrain, creating the Puget Sound basin and a mosaic of inland saltwater islands.

Younger than their cousins across Puget Sound, the Olympic Mountains dominate the landscape of the south Sound and the Olympic Peninsula. A towering fortress, the jagged peaks encircle deep forests of old growth and steep valleys laced with waterfalls and surging rivers. The heart of the Olympic peninsula remains remote and largely inaccessible by road; the mountains seemingly reserve entry only for those who would journey by foot. And, like the Cascades, the Olympic Mountains also create a unique set of climatic anomalies. Squeezed against their windward slopes, clouds moving inland off the ocean drop significant amounts of precipitation, making the Hoh River Valley a dense, temperate rainforest. Scarcely more than fifty miles away, in the mountains' rainshadow, the northeast peninsula and a distinct area of northern Puget Sound lay in a semi-arid sunbelt.

Although I photograph from time to time in the Rocky Mountains, the desert Southwest, and other locations out of state, it is the remarkable diversity of imagery in Washington State that keeps me close to home. Within a six hour driving radius I can photograph wind-swept ocean waves, capture luminous-green moss in a rainforest, witness a sunrise over a volcanic glacier, or take a close-up of a tumbleweed in the sand. My work in landscape photography is a study of relationships, not only between the visual elements and living systems that make up the natural world, but also, more importantly, our human relationship to them. This book emerged from a growing desire to express my perspective on this special place I've called home since birth.

It is true that over time the people of this state have shaped the face of this land. We have turned the soil, changed the course of its mightiest river, and built our cities and communities. In a more profound way, however, I think that this land has shaped us. We are a product of our environment. How does the landscape influence and impact those who live and work within it? I believe that each of us has a personal answer to that question.

I remember when my good friend, Rolf, returned home from Boston the summer of our nineteenth year. He had just won the assistant principal trumpet position of the Boston Symphony, outplaying in dramatic fashion the finest players in the country, most twice his age and experience, all coveting this prestigious position. The conductor chose him with great enthusiasm, exclaiming he had never heard a trumpet sound so big, rich, and glorious. As Rolf and I played duets one morning in his old bedroom, he recounted the details of his audition. I asked him innocently how he happened to develop such a big, full tone. He paused a moment, then raised his hand and motioned to Puget Sound and the Olympic Mountains rising in full view out his window. "Look," he mused, "how big a concert hall I had to fill with my sound," We laughed and kept playing, too young perhaps to understand the deeper truth of that simple observation.

As I have grown and experienced more of my life through the lens of a camera, I see more clearly than ever the profound relationship between who we are and where we live. I like to think of the magnificence of this land as a vision: a vision of the land which we see all around us, and a vision of our imagining, of considering the greater possibilities in our lives.

As one looks out across the landscape of our communities in this state, one sees an impressive gathering of people, ideas, and achievements of global significance. Washington is the spawning ground for innovation and success in the realms of aviation, high-tech scientific research, agriculture, forest products, and art, to name a few. I believe that people individually and collectively seldom venture far from the reach of their vision. As we look around this state, in the lives of its people, the vitality and richness of this land is expressed.

The images in this book represent my best work in the last ten years. Some places you may recognize, some may be a pleasant discovery. The beauty of our state is all around us, out our backdoor step, at our feet. Consequently, I went to no extraordinary lengths to photograph these images. In fact, most of them were taken standing on or alongside a road.

This is an exciting time to live in Washington, to participate in the unfolding and still developing vision that we hold for our state. I hope that you might find in these images a sense of a collective vision that we can all share; one that holds the promise of prosperity, and encourages us to nurture and protect the health of this land as we would nurture and protect our own well-being. In a very real way, they are one and the same.

WINTER

The steam rising from the boiling water on my portable stove felt good on my cold, cramped fingers. As soon as the coffee was done brewing, I could warm up the rest of me. Sipping from my mug, I walked along a trail down to the Sauk River, hoping the movement would loosen a body made stiff from a cold night's sleep. I had arrived at the campground late the night before, in anticipation that the forecast winter storm would leave some of its bounty here in the lower elevations. Standing at the shore and looking up, I noticed patches of blue sky appearing in the low cloud cover overhead.

Munching on granola and a green apple, I decided to drive back into Darrington; perhaps Whitehorse Mountain might be partially visible in this early morning light. From the outskirts of town I could see a sheer, jagged portion of the summit peaking through the clouds swirling around its face. Setting up my camera, I had no idea that the passing storm had dumped a record five feet on the Cascades during the night. One by one, the magenta rays of morning sun broke through the clouds and danced spiritedly across an emerging stage of lustrous powdered snow. By mid-morning the entire mountain appeared, looming majestically above the countryside, its new crown of white shimmering in the sun.

Packing up in a hurry, I drove back to the river, hoping that the light frosting of snow had not disappeared from the trees. As if my request had been granted, the low clouds still hung in the river valley, keeping the fire of sunlight from reaching the snow. Hiking up a steep trail through the woods, I followed a cascading, emerald tributary of the Sauk, my breath forming dense little clouds that hung stationary in the cold, damp air. A tapestry of ferns and drooping branches of moss, all etched in white, framed the creek like a wall hanging as I photographed it from above.

Farther down the Sauk River, I began looking for familiar spots along the Mountain Loop Highway. The winter days here may be gloomy and overcast, however, there is a richness of color and a subtle beauty that is very striking. And though nature may be in a state of rest, the lush, green beds of ferns, the leafless brown and orange stalks, the mosaic of opal colored rocks exposed in the riverbed, and the deep, intense hues of the river, are but a few of the visual elements that proclaim this land is very much alive.

Chilled to the bone and weary from the cold, I drug myself into the driver's seat to begin the trip home. I thought maybe I should have gone to Leavenworth where, although it is usually much colder, it might have been sunny. Yeah, but it's a dry cold, I told myself. The thought of the steamy, bubbling hot tub waiting for me at home made the journey seem shorter.

SPRING

Slipping off my shoes and rolling up my pants, I ventured into the water up to my knees. Grimacing from the numbing cold, I looked down. The clear, translucence of the shallow depth transitioned rapidly through hues of aqua, turquoise, teal and black-blue, as the lake bed dropped off dramatically in a relatively short distance. Spinning quickly, I returned to the comfort of shore in a few bounding leaps, my ritualistic reacquaintence with Crescent Lake duly performed.

I walked slowly along the top of the embankment, eyes fixed on the groupings of alders standing on the shore's edge. The delicate new leaves of pale green leapt out from the background of the intense, multi-hued lake below. I think this lake has more shades of blue than a designer's color card. Taking a break from photographing, I pulled my trumpet out to practice. I gazed at the scene before me as I warmed up and wondered, if these colors were music, what would they sound like? Playing to the rhythm of white-crested, blue waves lapping on the shore, I improvised a sweet but mournful tone poem.

Past the west end of the lake, I drove up the steep grade towards the Soleduck River Valley, nibbling on lunch as I went. Returning to this river often throughout the seasons, I have come to know it like the unique lines, expressions, and smile of a good friend's face. And like an enduring friendship, each new visit here reveals something I had not seen before. With the awakening of spring, the first trickles of snow-melt join company as they find their path down the glaciers and snow fields on the peaks high above the river. Standing on its bank, I listened to the music of a river running fast and deep. A few yards offshore, the large rock I sat on in the river's low ebb of late Autumn is but an abstract flicker of form beneath the rushing water. Tumbling, pirouetting, twisting, falling, the river celebrates a renewal of life. A dance of the river, its spirited voice sings, rejoicing in the emergence of another spring in the mountain valley.

Back on the shore of Crescent Lake, taking a deep breath, I made a flying leap, stretched out, belly flopping in the shallow water. Exhilarated by the tingling of my skin, I launched upward. Wiping the lake off my goose bumps, I looked westward. The fleeting orange rays of sunset cutting between the steep mountainsides bid farewell to another day with one last stroke of sunlight across the water. I, too, said good-bye with one last look, then turned and headed back to my van. Pulling out on the highway with the vision of a spring day at Crescent Lake fresh in my mind, I began to hum an arrangement to my new composition.

SUMMER

Waking suddenly, I turned over and looked up as the first waves of morning light washed inside of the van. Sliding the door back, I peered out across Banks Lake; the still water seemed on fire with the intense orange and red hues of a summer dawn. It was four-thirty a.m., and the last and brightest stars of the night sparkled in solitude against a sapphire sky, silhouetting the angular basalt cliffs rising on the distant shore. Securing the camera bag on my back, I set out to photograph the sunrise from a high ledge above the lake, wondering how it is that I always seem to wake up before the sunrise without an alarm. As I trudged along a narrow trail, disturbing the flora, a bouquet of the sweet, earthy scent of sage, native grasses, and dust, wafting up from the ground, grabbed hold of my senses, awakening me like no latte ever did. Arriving at my spot, I began to set up my tripod. Perched motionless atop a rock in the lake, a graceful blue heron looked like an elegant Japanese ink drawing reflected in the water below me. I photographed the rugged cliffs and small islands in the lake for hours, changing positions and subjects as the transmuting light of the rising sun brush-stroked new forms and colors with each passing moment.

The beauty of this arid landscape derives from its vast open spaces, and a sense of the almost unimaginable natural forces and passing of time that sculpted this starkly dramatic visual masterpiece. Here, the earth bares itself to the transformative elements of wind, rain, snow, and sunlight. It is a dance of life that plays out through the millennium, and before the naked eye. Sometimes it is hard to tell where the earth stops and the sky begins, for here they seem as one.

Leaving the lake and driving north towards Grand Coulee Dam, I was reminded of another significant force of nature. It was the energy and imagination of our species that harnessed the Columbia River, and flooded a sweeping landscape of sagebrush and jackrabbits that we now call Banks Lake. However, unlike the gradual but inexorable processes of nature, we unleashed the potent forces of technology, creating a new landscape in but a flicker of geologic time. Stopping for gas, I spied an espresso stand across the highway. Perhaps I'd have that latte after all.

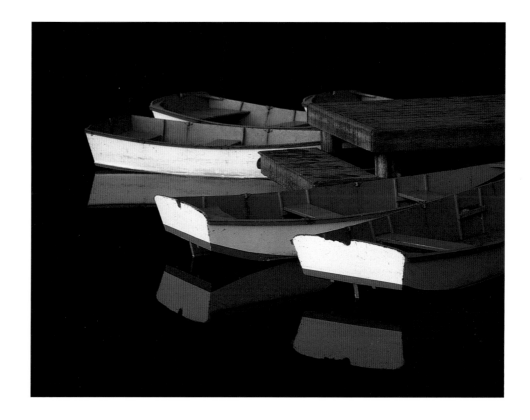

AUTUMN

Driving down the on-ramp, I shifted into fourth and turned on KING FM, hoping a little Mozart might help me organize my presentation later that morning. "Low clouds and fog in the Puget Sound area, with the freezing level dropping to 1500 feet in the Cascades later today," announcer Tom Olsen said. I had been keeping close track of the progression of color changes since the last week of September, like I always do, and now, at the fifth of October, the unusually cool weather was accelerating the seasonal transition noticeably.

Looking past the Montlake Bridge and Husky Stadium as I drove I-5 over the Ship Canal, I saw heavy dark clouds shrouding all but the lowest foothills of the Cascades. I looked at my watch and knew it was time for an executive decision: continue to my meeting or head over the Evergreen Point Bridge, grab my gear at home, and get into the mountains as fast as I could to photograph the snowfall. Running out my front door twenty minutes later, I thought I had better call and cancel the meeting. As I rumbled through Sultan, the lifting clouds revealed the distinct edge of a fresh snowline glistening in a laser beam of sunlight. Any lingering doubts about my change of schedule were fast melting away with each mile.

Actually, the rare opportunity to photograph an early autumn snowfall requires no decision at all: it simply can not be missed. Winding up Stevens Pass Highway, I glanced intermittently across the road, inspecting the shore of the Skykomish River for photographic possibilities. Embroidered with a delicate lace of white, the collage of big leaf and vine maple, trunks of red alder, and drooping moss, appeared as a soft, abstract watercolor. Stopping to shoot only briefly at several points on the journey to the summit, I apportioned my time carefully, for down the crest on the eastern slopes lay a landscape of another beauty. Golden fields of grasses, pine trees, and the brilliant saturated hues of the leaves of birch and aspen composed a portrait of autumn that stunned the senses. Near Lake Wenatchee, toward Tumwater Canyon, the creeping fog and reflected light from the dusting of snow combined to create an almost surreal, unbroken palette of muted colors as my eyes panned in all directions.

After photographing until there was not enough light to get a meter reading, I threw my camera bag in the van and set out for home. Driving back over the summit in a downpour, I marveled at the two very distinct visions of a Washington autumn I had captured on film in the course of but a few short, harried hours. Tomorrow morning, I thought, I will reschedule that meeting.

PLATES